CW01574400

WRITTEN BY

ODILE BREAUD AND SYLVIE ASSATHIANY,
JOELLE BUSUTTIL, ANNE DE HENNING,
CHANTAL HENRY-BIABAUD, LAURENCE OTTENHEIMER,
BERNARD PLANCHE, PENNY STANLEY-BAKER

ILLUSTRATED BY

NICOLE BARON, DANIELE BOUR, CHRISTIAN BROUTIN,
BEAT BRUSCH, BERNARD DAGAN, PIERRE DENIEUIL, LUC FAVREAU,
BRUNO FOURURE, HENRI GALERON, DONALD GRANT, CLAUDE AND DENISE MILLET,
MICHELLE NICKLY, JEAN-MARIE POISSENOT, LAURENCE QUENTIN, RENE METTLER, ALINE RIQUIER,
JACQUES ROZIER AND MONIQUE GAUDRIAULT, ETIENNE SOUPPART,
VALERIE STETTEN, PIERRE-MARIE VALAT

TRANSLATED AND ADAPTED BY

SCOTT STEEDMAN
WITH SARAH MATTHEWS, SARAH GIBSON,
PENNY STANLEY-BAKER AND SUE BIRCHENALL

We gratefully acknowledge the advice of:
The Embassy of the Republic of Zaïre in the UK,
Professor H.T. Norris, The School of Oriental and African Studies, University of London,
Dr John Mack, African Curator, The Museum of Mankind, London,
Australian High Commission, London,
Indian High Commission, London,
David Rootes, Polar Consultant

Cover design by Peter Bennett

ISBN 1 85103 177 4
© 1990 by Editions Gallimard
English text © 1993
by Moonlight Publishing Ltd
First published in Great Britain 1993 by Moonlight Publishing Ltd,
36 Stratford Road, London W8
Printed in Italy by Editoriale Libraria

LIVING AROUND THE WORLD

CONTENTS

MOONLIGHT PUBLISHING

Europe – a small, crowded continent...

Would you like to travel across the five continents? To begin with, here is Europe, the smallest one! If you look at a map of the world, you can see that Europe and Asia form a single, vast territory unbroken by seas or deserts. Part of Russia is in Europe, the other part in Asia.
Do you know where the name Europe comes from? She is the heroine of a Greek legend. Zeus, king of the gods, fell in love with her and carried her to an island in the Mediterranean. European civilization* was born on the shores of this sea.

Seven hundred million people live in the 37 countries that make up Europe. That's a lot for such a small area! But the population of Europe is not increasing as fast as the rest of the world's population.

Many people set sail from Europe to settle in other countries.

Twelve European countries are united in the European Community, or EC.

In Norway, mountains run straight into the sea in fjords.

The coast of Western Europe, beaten by the Atlantic Ocean.

Most of Europe has a temperate climate, which means that it is rarely too cold or too hot. Few areas are uninhabitable. Of course, people who make their homes near the Arctic* Circle don't live the same way as those on the Mediterranean coast! In the extreme north, in Norway and Finland, winter lasts for seven or eight months. The Baltic Sea freezes over. At the same time, in the south, orange trees are in fruit.

On the shores of the Atlantic Ocean, summer and winter are similar. Both are mild and often rainy. This is the climate of Ireland, Britain and the west of France. These areas are green and grassy.

In Central Europe, in Poland, Hungary, and the Czech and Slovak republics, the climate is continental. Seasons are marked: winters are cold, summers are hot.

A southern European landscape, under the blazing sun

The high, rocky peaks of the Carpathians, in Central Europe

Homes for the heat, homes for the cold

What are houses like in Europe?
They vary from country to country and even from region to region.
In Greece, to keep out the heat and brilliant sunshine of summer, the houses have tiny windows and thick walls painted bright white. Every spring, people whitewash their homes in preparation for the coming summer. White reflects the heat and the house stays cool inside.

Windmills, with sails or wooden blades , aren't just used to grind flour. In Holland, they drive pumps which draw water through the canals. In Greece, they are still used to press oil out of olives.

In the north of Europe, in Scandinavia, huge areas are still covered in great forests of pine and birch trees.

So houses there are built of wood, often painted bright red or yellow.
In the west of Europe, in Brittany and Normandy in France and in the south-west of England, a hard rock called granite is found in huge outcrops. It is easy to recognize because it shines in the rain. Here many houses are made of granite.

Red roofs and grey roofs
In the south, roofs are usually covered with red clay tiles that have been fired in a kiln. Mountain chalets are protected by slate, a heavy rock that breaks into fine slivers. Slate roofs resist violent winds very well.

A world of variety in one small continent

Customs, clothing and ways of life differ from one place to another, too.
In Europe, only the British and the Irish drive on the left side of the road!
Europe measures its goods in metres, kilos and litres, using the metric system.
Britain is now gradually moving towards the metric system too.
Because of the heat, Italians and Spaniards take a siesta* in the middle of the day.
Shops close until four or five o'clock, then stay open late into the night, when the air is cool and pleasant. The evening is also the time to go for a stroll in southern Europe. This evening walk is called the 'paseo' in Spain, the 'passeggiata' in Italy... People wander up and down in the shade of the boulevards, saying hello to friends, exchanging gossip.

Every country in Europe has its own language.
Some have more than one. Many of these languages are similar, because they share the same Latin, Anglo-Saxon or Slav roots.

In Mediterranean countries, the markets open first thing in the morning, while the air is still cool and fresh.

In many parts of Britain, the milkman delivers milk to your doorstep every morning.

The canals of Amsterdam reflect the gables of the brick houses.

In France, there is a bakery in every village. Here the people can buy fresh bread every day, from early in the morning.

Costumes, celebrations and customs have been passed down the centuries.

Some celebrations take place all over Europe; others are restricted to a single country. In France, 14 July is Bastille Day: the French commemorate the Revolution. In London, on the Queen's official birthday, there is the Trooping of the Colour. Christians across Europe celebrate Easter and Christmas; Jews observe Yom Kippur and Hanukkah; Muslims fast for Ramadan.

Shepherds on mountain pastures high in the Alps and the Pyrenees still wear traditional clothes.

Dancer from Andalusia, in Spain

Hungarian boy

Swedish costume for the festival of St Lucia

Eggs, flying bells and a bunny – it must be Easter!

Did you know that in France, children believe that Easter eggs are left in the garden by bells that fly from Rome?
In Britain, Germany and Austria, they are brought by an Easter bunny who dashes about with his basket under his arm.
In Orthodox Christian countries like Russia and Bulgaria, people paint eggs at Easter.

In Europe, you can celebrate Christmas from 6 December to 6 January.

The children of Belgium and some parts of Germany don't have to wait until 25 December, Christmas Day, to get their presents. St Nicholas (Santa Claus) comes to visit them on 6 December, dressed as a bishop.
In Scandinavia, the holidays begin on 13 December, the festival of St Lucia.
In darkest winter, they celebrate the Festival of Light. The youngest girl in the house wakes up everyone else and gives them oranges and sweets.
Young Italians wait eagerly for 6 January, the Day of the Kings, when they are visited by 'Befana', an old fairy godmother who brings them toys.

Every country has its own foods and ways of cooking.

Camembert, France | Quark, Germany | Parmesan, Italy | Manchego, Spain | Gorgonzola, Italy | Double Gloucester, England | Tilsit, Germany

Nowadays most people in Europe have enough to eat. This hasn't always been true. In the Middle Ages, for example, food shortages and famines killed thousands. Even today, some countries have problems feeding all their people. In parts of central and eastern Europe, the shop shelves are often empty. People have to stand in queues for hours, just to buy a loaf of bread.

Have you ever tasted any of these dishes?
Here are some Dutch cheese and broodjes (bread rolls); stuffed vine leaves and kebabs from Greece; a French potée (hot pot) with a baguette (bread stick); mussels and chips from Belgium...

<u>To each his own... every country has specialities.</u>
In Germany, the variety of breads is endless: they are made with every sort of cereal. Italy is the home of pasta, and the best place for coffee. France is well known for its wine and its cheeses. Britain is renowned for its puddings and its excellent meat. Gruyère cheese comes from Switzerland; Gouda, from the Netherlands.

...roll-mops (herrings) from Denmark; Spanish paella (a rice and seafood dish); cold meats, pretzels and sauerkraut from Germany; a British breakfast of porridge, bacon and eggs; spaghetti and pizza from Italy and baked cod from Portugal.

North America used to be called the New World.

To the west of Europe, across the Atlantic Ocean, lies North America. Its first inhabitants arrived there from Asia more than 20,000 years ago. Over the centuries they split into tribes, each with its own customs and traditions. They farmed, hunted and fished, in the forests and across the plains. During the sixteenth century the first Europeans came to North America. Because they thought this unknown land was Asia, they called the native Americans Indians.

Persecuted for their religious beliefs or tired of living in poverty, many Europeans went to start a new life in North America.
At first they settled on the coast, but soon they began to explore the interior, in search of new land to settle and farm.
The settlers and their families headed west in groups of covered wagons. The men rode with guns to keep guard, the women drove the teams of horses.
Once they had found a place to build their homesteads, the pioneers raised large herds of cattle. The men who looked after these herds were cowboys.

Soon the settlements threatened the survival of the native Americans, and bitter battles were fought as the Indians struggled to keep their lands. Eventually they were forced to abandon their traditional way of life and move on to the small reservations set aside for them by the invaders.

Canada, a land of forests and a million lakes

Across the north of America lies Canada, a huge country 40 times bigger than Britain. But it has less than half the population. Most of the land is covered in lakes and forests. Canada's forests provide nearly half the world's wood, and countless tonnes of pulp for making paper. Summers are very hot and winters are bitterly cold. The big, bustling cities are all by rivers and lakes in the milder south.

Canada has two official languages, French and English. Many people are immigrants* and speak Chinese, Punjabi, Ukrainian…

In spring it is time to collect the sap of maple trees. Canadians boil this up to make a sweet syrup like honey. It is delicious on pancakes! The maple leaf is the symbol of Canada, found on the flag.

If polar bears in the far north of Canada don't find enough to eat during the summer, they come into town and raid rubbish bins.

There are fifty separate states in the USA.

Many American houses
are made of wood that comes from the country's forests.

They usually have a garage for the car, and a garden.

Children make a little pocket-money by washing cars or helping in the garden.

The postman brings the letters by car.

South of Canada is the United States of America.
Do you know where the USA gets its name? It is made up of fifty states which came together to form one huge country.

Every morning before school, pupils and teachers salute the American flag.

The fifty stars on the American flag represent all the different states. Each state has its own laws and its own capital. Nowadays the United States is one of the most powerful countries in the world.

From the Atlantic coast to the Pacific coast, people are living the American way.
Only a few are native American Indians; most are descendants of settlers or immigrants* who have come to the United States of America from all over the world. Most people speak English, but it sounds very different from the English spoken in Britain. Spanish is also widely spoken.

School days and days for dressing up

Early in the morning, big yellow buses criss-cross the cities and towns, picking up children.

A day at school

American schools are often on the edge of a city or town, surrounded by forests or countryside.

Every pupil carries a little lunch-box with sandwiches and fruit inside. Some bring a thermos full of tea, or a bottle of Coke. At lunch-time, the children sit in the classroom or playground and have a picnic. Some schools give the pupils little bottles of milk to drink with their lunch.

American children drink lots of milk! They have a glass with breakfast, to go with a big plate of pancakes or waffles, a bowl of cereal or porridge, scrambled eggs, sausages… After school, it's time for a glass of milk and perhaps a couple of chocolate-chip cookies.

In the USA and Canada, ice hockey is the most popular winter sport. In summer, children play baseball in parks.

31 October: Hallowe'en, when the witches and the goblins come out

Everyone dresses up as clowns, ghosts, witches, vampires... The monsters go from door to door saying "Trick or Treat", collecting sweets in bags.

In front of every house, big pumpkins with carved faces, lit by candles, keep an eye on the ghostly parade…

In the USA, everything is big.

In the summer, families take off with their caravans or tents to explore the huge natural parks of the American West.

Alaska, to the north of Canada, is another American state.

This immense country includes every habitat you can imagine, from scorching deserts to glistening ice-fields.

The Pacific coast has thousands of kilometres of rocky shores and sandy beaches. In the north-west, most of the beaches are deserted.

In Arizona, where the Navaho Indians live on reservations, huge islands of stone jut out of the red rock of the desert.

New York, a jungle of skyscrapers

The White House, Washington DC.
The President of the USA works here.

George Washington gave his name to the capital of the United States.
He had fought for independence from the British and became the first president in 1789. Bill Clinton was elected the 42nd President in 1992.

New York is the biggest, busiest city.
It is a bustling centre of banks, museums and theatres. Wide streets run in straight lines up and down the crowded island of Manhattan. Skyscrapers almost hide the sky from view.

San Francisco, on the Pacific coast, is built on 43 hills.

South and Central America, where so many races meet

The other part of the American continent stretches from Mexico in the north to Tierra del Fuego, the southern tip of the world. The people here speak Spanish or, in Brazil, Portuguese. Many Central and South Americans are also part or pure American Indian and speak one of the many Indian languages.

The southern continent, like the northern, was first inhabited by Indians. Their empires rose and fell: the last great ones were those of the Aztecs and Mayas in Central America and the Incas in South America. These rich and powerful tribes prospered for centuries. They were skilled craftsmen and engineers. Their statues, temples and pyramids can still be seen in Mexico and Peru.

The emperor of the Incas was said to be descended from the Sun God.

In the 15th century, Spanish and Portuguese explorers crossed the sea in their galleons in search of Eldorado – 'the golden one' – and arrived on the South American coast. They ruthlessly invaded the Indian territories, destroying their great civilizations and stealing their treasures.

Soon after these conquistadores* came ships full of European settlers. These new South Americans made their first homes along the Atlantic coast, then moved further and further inland.

The magnificent Iguaçu Falls, on the border between Argentina and Brazil

From tropical beaches to the windswept tip of Tierra del Fuego

A mixed population

Over centuries, more settlers came from Europe. The population is still divided into three main groups: descendants of European settlers, native South American Indians, and mestizos, people of both Indian and European blood. Descendants of African slaves brought by Europeans form a fourth group.

High mountains, steamy jungles, sandy beaches

To the west, the rugged Andes range rises like a rampart, crowned with fields of ice and snow. In the centre the Amazon, the biggest river in the world, crosses a huge jungle, the Amazon rainforest. On the other side of the continent, the warm waters of thc Caribbean Sea lap sandy beaches on the coast of Venezuela.

To the south are the grassy pampas, home to cattle and the cowboys, or gauchos*, who herd them. At the tip lie Patagonia and Tierra del Fuego – 'the land of fire'. In this dry, windswept landscape, no trees grow.

The jagged peaks of the Andes mountain range

The condor and the llama live high in the Andes Mountains.

Along the Venezuelan coast, the water can be crystal clear.

Cape Horn, the barren, southern tip of the continent

Mexico, baked under the hot, tropical sun

Mexico's capital is the biggest city in the world.
Mexico City, one of the world's highest cities, is nearly two kilometres above sea level. It was built beside the ruins of the ancient Indian capital, Teotihuacan, 'city of the gods', which flourished 1,400 years ago. The thousands of factories in Mexico City are the source of much of the city's wealth, pollution and misery. Many workers come to the city from the countryside and live in shanty towns in desperate poverty. Friendly and welcoming, Mexicans love festivals and carnivals. There is music everywhere; in the cool of the evening, to the sound of the guitar, people sing of their hopes and dreams. In grand processions, trumpets blare to celebrate the saint who protects each village. On the Day of the Dead, 1 November, people visit the graves of their friends and relatives. That evening they dress up like skeletons and dance in the streets.

Two Mexican specialities: tortillas, pancakes made from cornflour, and frozen fruit: pineapple, guava, papaya.

Mexico is a mixture of Spanish, Indian and American influences.
There are traces of each culture. Temples and palaces of the Mayas and the Aztecs still stand, deep in the jungle or high in the mountains. The Spanish built white churches where Mexicans still worship on Sundays.
Modern banks, shopping malls and skyscrapers are designed to withstand earthquakes, which often shake Mexico.

To protect your head from the strong tropical sun, what better than a sombrero? These incredibly wide straw hats are only worn by men.

Most Mexicans have been Roman Catholics since the conquistadores* arrived. They honour many saints. Some say that the old Aztec gods have even become saints...

The Andes are home to Indians, descendants of the Incas.

South of Mexico, America is so narrow that the Panama Canal has been dug right across it.

Boats cross from the Atlantic to the Pacific and back again, without having to sail all the way round the continent.

To the south is South America, made up of thirteen countries. Under the snowy peaks of the Andes Mountains, between three and five thousand metres, is a land of high plateaux. This is the last home of the Indians, descendants of the mighty Incas.

In the high Andes, each tribe has its own colourful costumes, traditions and customs. You can tell them apart by the shapes of the hats the women wear.

Women also wear bright, baggy skirts, one on top of the other, the oldest ones on the bottom, and ponchos, wool shawls that they weave by hand.

Meals are often eaten outdoors.

The food is spicy, seasoned with hot peppers and coriander, and based on maize, potatoes and tomatoes – three plants that the Indians discovered.

Brazil takes up half of South America.

The 'capoeira', a stylized imitation of a fight, is a traditional dance in the region called Salvador de Bahia.

From Bahia to Rio, from São Paulo to Brasilia, the cities of Brazil are all so different.

Rio de Janeiro is a very lively city built around a wide and beautiful bay.
Its endless beaches are broken by rocky outcrops that jut out like giant teeth.
The inhabitants of Rio, who call themselves Cariocas, are very proud of their city and especially its famous beaches: Ipanema, Copacabana, Leblon.
Imagine kilometres of white sand where you can ride your bike, go for a stroll, or even, if you're feeling brave, take a swim.

Brasilia, the new capital of Brazil, was built in four years in the middle of the desert.

These candles are Macumbas, offerings to the goddess of the sea.

Salvador de Bahia, further north along the coast, is a grim reminder of Brazil's history. Here African men, women and children were unloaded from ships and forced to work as slaves on sugar-cane plantations, until slavery became illegal in the nineteenth century.
Many Brazilians are descended from African families.

Brazil is a land of many contrasts.

Houses made of sheet metal

Clinging to the hills of Rio are endless favelas, or slum* towns. The thousands of small houses are little more than sheets of corrugated iron riveted together.
Life is hard for the families here.
The children earn a little money selling ice-cream or fruit juice on the beach.

On the north coast of Brazil,
where the white sandy beaches seem to go on forever, the children carry home the fish their fathers have caught from 'jangadas', strange windsurfers. The fishermen go out to sea in twos or threes, standing up.
When night falls, they lash themselves to the boat and sleep at sea, out of sight of land. In the morning, the cool breezes carry them back to the beach.

São Paulo, in the south of Brazil, is the country's coffee capital.
It has become a thriving business centre bursting with traffic and noise, a chaotic jungle of skyscrapers and motorways.
There is even an airport right in the middle of the city.
The population of São Paulo is increasing so quickly that they can't build schools fast enough. The same rooms have to hold two, sometimes even three classes side by side, day after day.

Cuzco was the capital of the Inca empire.

Cuzco is in Peru, a high country on the west coast of South America.
It is one of the highest cities in the world, perched in the heart of the Andes. To get there you catch a little train that climbs to more than 5,000 metres, higher than any mountain in Europe.
The passengers feel dizzy as they breathe the thin mountain air.
Cuzco was the capital of the Inca empire, which ruled ten million people. It means 'centre of the world'.

Women come to Cuzco from near and far to sell vegetables and poultry in the market. Others stand on street corners selling mango, banana or papaya juice to people passing by.
The days are clear and sunny and the nights are very cold. The temperature can drop twenty-five degrees when the sun sets.

Further south, vast plains stretch to the horizon in all directions. These plains are the pampas – like North America's prairies, they are grasslands where huge herds of cattle roam. They are tended by gauchos* who work on vast farms, called 'haciendas' in Argentina, 'fazendas' in Brazil. They ride great distances over the windy, treeless pampas, watching out for swamps and bogs. The gaucho rides high in his saddle, his feet never touching the ground. He catches cattle with a lasso without getting off his horse.

The cowboys of South America, the gauchos*, cook their fresh meat over open fires on the pampas.

Stone walls built by the Incas still stand. Though the stones were put together without mortar, they remain secure.

The Amazon River flows for 7,000 kilometres through tropical rainforest.

If you were to look down on South America at the Equator, you would see nothing but green in all directions. This is the immense Amazon rainforest, an endless jungle, fed by the mighty Amazon River.

Here and there, lone houses stand on stilts over the river. They are the homes of Indians. The people go everywhere by boat. Even the Incas could not conquer these proud tribes who live in the dense jungle.

The Sahara Desert cuts Africa in two.

Millions of years ago, Africa and South America were joined as one big continent. The two were slowly pulled apart, and the Atlantic Ocean poured into the gap between them. More recently, a million years ago, the first humans appeared in Africa, before spreading to the other continents.

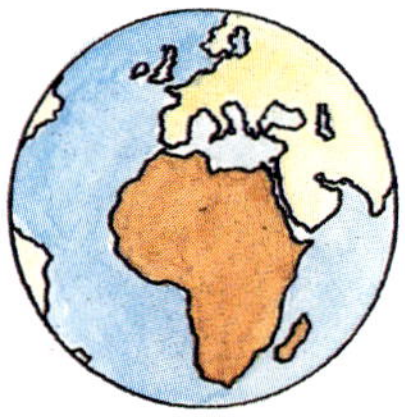

Africans living in the lands north of the Sahara traded with Europeans and shared cultural influences. South of the Sahara, however, the great kingdoms of Mali, Benin and Zimbabwe remained unknown to the rest of the world until Europeans began to explore the west coast in the 1400s and finally penetrated the interior in the late nineteenth century. Most of Africa was controlled by Europeans until the 1950s, but now many African peoples have regained independence.

A village market where nomads* sell their animals

Grasslands and rainforests support a rich variety of wildlife.

The vast Sahara in the north is the largest desert in the world, about the size of the USA. In the south-east lies another desert, just as dry, just as fascinating: the Kalahari. Millions of years ago, the Sahara was green and fertile. But the climate began to change; less and less rain fell, and the land dried up. Slowly, the desert is spreading across Africa.

Nearer the Equator*, it rains more. Grass covers the plains, thorny trees and bushes give a little shade. This is the savanna*. Close to the Equator, in the heart of Africa, the skies are often cloudy and it rains a lot. Trees and plants love the warm, steamy air, and dense rainforests cover the hills and valleys.

The Tuareg people are always on the move.

Little boys have their hair shaved off. Teenage boys grow theirs into plaits.

The Tuareg are nomads*.
They raise camels, cattle, sheep and goats on the fringes of the Sahara Desert. The Tuareg are constantly on the move, because after a few weeks there is nothing left for their animals to graze on. The families roll up their tents, collect their belongings, and move on.

In the desert, finding water is everyone's main priority.
Each morning, the women trudge several kilometres to fill their goatskins at the well. Water from the well has to be hauled up by a camel, or by a team of strong men, because the well-bucket holds 40 litres and the well is about 60 metres deep.

Traditionally the Tuareg live in tents.
Everyone in the camp is related, but each family – usually a man, his wife and their children – lives in a separate tent. It takes about thirty goatskins, tanned and stitched together, to make a tent. The roof is low, so you can't stand up inside. Everyone sleeps on a big platform, apart from the older boys who sleep out under the stars.

The goatskin bag is smeared with butter to make it waterproof.

Tuareg children learn Arabic and French
when they go to school. Their parents teach them to speak and write in Tuareg, which has its own special alphabet. Instead of using paper, the children write in the desert sand.

The women have to wait their turn at the well. Shepherds from other camps are there too, fetching water for their animals. The well is a meeting-place; people chat and exchange news.

The Tuareg cook outdoors, on camp fires. Meals are usually millet porridge or pancakes made from wheat flour, with fresh or curdled goats' milk, and sometimes a few dates.

They drink a lot of sweet tea. When visitors come, they are welcomed with several glasses of tea.

In the evening, inside the tent, women play the imzad, a sort of violin.

To protect themselves from sun and wind, the Tuareg wear long, loose robes. These are dyed blue and the Tuareg are called 'blue men' because the colour stains their skin. Men wrap their heads so that you only see their eyes – they never show their faces to strangers or important members of their families. Women don't wear veils, but they sometimes cover their mouths as a sign of respect.

In the thick of the forest, a Central African village

<u>**Here is a village in the heart of Africa.**</u> Houses are built of clay bricks dried in the sun and are thatched with palm leaves. The men cut down trees and clear the undergrowth with machetes* to make room for houses and crops. The women plant vegetables like cassava, maize and yams. There's firewood to collect, washing to be done in the river and water to be fetched...
The women are good at balancing heavy loads on their heads.
It's a long, hard day under the hot, African sun.
The men catch fish and hunt monkeys and crocodiles, which make a delicious stew for the evening meal.

People go to the village headman to sort out their problems and arguments.

School days and market days

What's it like growing up in an African village?
Even quite young children have to learn to help their parents with everyday chores. The girls help crush the cassava roots into a sort of flour, called chikwangue. They roll the chikwangue into little balls, wrap it in banana leaves, and steam it over an open fire. These dumplings are very good for mopping up gravy!

Women wrap their babies in lengths of cloth and carry them at their hips.

The boys learn to fish and to hunt with a bow. Their fathers teach them how to copy the calls of different birds and other animals, to lure them into traps.

What about school?
There isn't a school in every village. Children aged between 6 and 12 often have to walk for an hour or two each morning to reach the primary school some miles away. If there is no school building, lessons take place outside under a tree.

These children are learning French.

Market day is a time to meet friends and talk, as well as to buy and sell. Goods are laid out on the ground on pieces of cloth. There are fruits like mangoes, pineapples, papayas, bananas, coconuts… There are vegetables too: cassava, sweet potatoes, chilli peppers.

Drums beat out the dance rhythm on days of celebration.

Everyone in this village in Zaïre joins in when there's something to celebrate.
It might be a wedding, the birth of a baby, or a good harvest. The dancers put on wooden masks and feathered head-dresses, and paint patterns on their skins. Drums beat out the rhythm and the fun begins! The dancing lasts all night.
Each village has its own special dance, with a name like 'Dance of Victory' or 'Dance of Lightning'.

There's not much time for playing, but it's fun to kick a ball around or make a car out of wire or wood.

Right in the heart of the Central African rainforest live the pygmies, an isolated race of people who have kept their ancient way of life. They know every secret of the forest even which plant makes good toothpaste! Pygmies are not very tall: even the men don't grow to more than about 1.5 metres. They hunt and fish, and gather fruit and nuts. They are fine musicians and dancers.

The most skilful fishermen are the Wagenia.
They drop long, reed baskets into the water. If a fish swims into a basket, it gets trapped in the narrow end and can't escape. Sometimes the catch is really big: a catfish can weigh as much as 90 kilos – enough to feed the whole village.

Modern cities attract people from the country.

Kinshasa is the capital of Zaïre, in Central Africa. It stretches across the Zaïre River, the longest river in Central Africa. Imagine blue sky, hot sun, and the smell of diesel oil and fish. Air-conditioned blocks of flats tower over slums. Motorways turn into dirt tracks. Bicycle bells jingle, lorries hoot, radios compete with the beat of drums.
The city is growing in all directions. People chatter and call to one another as buses arrive at the water's edge. Canoes jostle around the ships moored at the quay.

People come from the countryside by bus or boat. They come in search of work on building sites or in offices. But many find that there is poverty and hunger in the city, too. They do anything they can to make a little money: selling postcards, watermelons, cigarettes one by one, waiting to find a better job.

Many parents make long journeys to take their children to school. At the end of the day, the school children, often in uniform, pour into the city streets in their hundreds, chattering and laughing.

Asia is the most populated continent.

Asia: the word is full of magic. There is mystery and wonder in this great continent that is home to millions and millions of people, from Turkey to the farthest reaches of China, from Siberia to Borneo.
Jesus, Buddha, Mohammed... the great religions were all born here: Christianity, Islam, and earlier Judaism, Buddhism and Hinduism.
Writing was invented in Asia, thousands of years ago. So were arithmetic, astronomy, music, cartography and chemistry.

Camels, antelopes and lions in the savanna*

Half the world's people live in Asia.
But some regions are densely populated, while others are almost deserted.
Great natural barriers like the Himalayan Mountains, the world's highest peaks, and inhospitable deserts like the Gobi in China separate and isolate the many different civilizations: Arab, Indian, Chinese, Japanese, Thai...
To the north lies Siberia, frozen in winter, sweltering in summer. The west and centre are dominated by steppes* and deserts.

Elephants, herons, macaque monkeys and wild buffaloes live by the river's edge.

In the south, the winds of the monsoon control the rhythm of life.
In winter, they blow towards the sea and keep the land dry. In summer, they blow across the ocean and on to the land, bringing torrential rains that water the rice paddies, turning the fields green.

The jungle in the Bengal Delta is home to cobras, deer, rhinoceroses, storks, crocodiles, monkeys and tigers.

So many different landscapes, so many different Asians

A farmer from Laos. His turban protects him from the sun as he works in rice fields stepped in terraces.

A proud Afghan. Long caravans of camels cross Afghanistan to link Iran and Pakistan.

In Vietnam, the farmers work their rice paddies with the help of water buffaloes.

A Turk in front of St Sophia in Istanbul. This ancient Christian cathedral was turned into a mosque* when Istanbul fell to the Ottoman Turks in 1453.

The nomadic* Khirgiz people shelter in tents made of yak hides.

In India, a Mogul emperor had the Taj Mahal built in memory of his wife. It is made of white marble decorated with gemstones.

Many of China's great rivers have colour names. This junk, a traditional boat, is sailing down the Yangtze, or Blue River.

Oil is pumped from beneath the desert sands of Arabia. They call it black gold.

The Tibetans live on the roof of the world, in the Himalayas.

The Wailing Wall in Jerusalem, Israel

Russia, shared between Europe and Asia

The colourful bulbs of St Basil's Church dominate Red Square in Moscow, where the Communist Party ruled from the Kremlin.

Russia is more than twice the size of the USA. Until 1991, it was the biggest province in the USSR or Soviet Union. The Soviet Communist Party ruled the whole country. Now Russia's many neighbours are independent countries: Estonia, Belorussia, the Ukraine, Kazakhstan, Mongolia... A quarter of Russia lies in Europe, which ends at the feet of the Ural and Caucasus Mountains. Beyond stretches Asia: from the steppes of the centre to the frozen tundra of Siberia, from Armenia to Mongolia. If you caught a train in Moscow, the capital, it would take you seven days and seven nights to reach Vladivostok, on the Sea of Japan!

The immense steppes* of Kazakhstan disappear to the horizon in every direction. Only their edges are inhabited.

From icy Siberia to the deserts of Mongolia

The Trans-Siberian Express, the world's longest railway, crosses Siberia, where the climate is very harsh; it reaches minus 60°C in winter, and more than 40°C in summer.

Most Russians live in Europe, but recently many have moved to Siberia to work in huge mines and oil and gas fields. More than a hundred languages are spoken in Russia, but Russian is the most common. The letters are different from ours; Russian uses the Cyrillic alphabet, based on Greek.

Daily life is hard for many Russians. Because of the country's economic problems, even basic essentials are very expensive and usually in short supply. In towns, the shops are often empty, and people sometimes have to queue for hours to buy staple foods like bread and milk.

In the barren forests and deserts of Mongolia, nomads* shelter under tents of heavy canvas.

India: a land of colours and contrasts

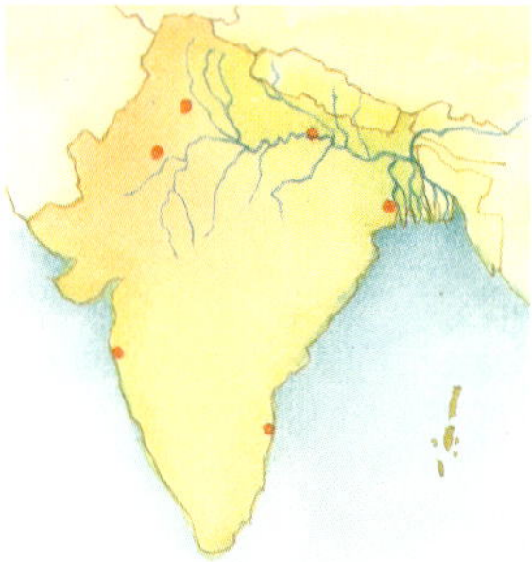

This is India, home to seven hundred thousand million people. This huge peninsula runs from the great Himalayan Mountains to the Indian Ocean. There are many different kinds of country: deserts, plains, jungles... Most Indians live in the countryside, but the cities and towns are overflowing.

A village in Rajasthan, in the north-west

In Rajasthan, the farmers tend goats and camels. The climate is dry. The walls of the houses are a mixture of mud and straw, dried in the hot sun. Roofs are thatched. The peasants sleep on string beds and keep their belongings in painted tin trunks.

In Kerala, a region of rice-fields and spice plantations, children go to school by boat. The sea weaves its inlets in and out of the land. People travel by boat along the canals and lagoons. There are many fishermen.

Everyone waits for the monsoon.

The wind is beginning to blow. Clouds are scudding across the sky. Then rain starts to fall, more and more of it, and storms flash and rumble.

This is the monsoon, when the rains come and water soaks the earth which has been baked dry by months of sunshine. Though many fields are now irrigated, the monsoon is still very important. Without it the farmers would have little to harvest and they would go hungry. But if the monsoon is too violent, then the crops are damaged, and that also means not enough to eat.

Life is reborn in the monsoon rains. Palm trees buckle in the wind and rice fields are flooded. The great rivers of India, the Ganges, Indus, Krishna and Brahmaputra, burst their banks and flood the nearby land.

After the monsoon has passed, winter sets in. In the north, the nights are cold, and people wrap up well to keep warm. In the south, winter is mild.

Summer starts around the end of March. By May it is so hot that the tar melts on the roadways. In the houses, big fans make a cooling draught. At night, people sleep out of doors.

How do Indians eat? With the fingers of the right hand. Meals are usually eaten with rice, or with cakes of wheat or millet called chapattis, which are used to pick up the vegetables or meat. There are many different curries, spicy stews of meat, fish or vegetables.

Women wear a sari. This is a brightly coloured piece of silk or cotton cloth five and a half metres long, wrapped around the waist and draped over the left shoulder. The men wear a kurta, a collarless shirt, over churidar, tight cotton trousers, or over a dhoti, a length of cloth wrapped round the waist and tucked between the legs.

An Indian wedding lasts several days.

The bridegroom may arrive at his fiancée's house on a beautifully dressed horse, accompanied by a younger brother or sister.

A marriage is an important event in Indian society. Parents are involved in choosing a partner for their son or daughter. In Rajasthan, the ceremony takes place at night at the bride's house. The bride and groom, dressed in the finest silk and brocade, walk seven times round a holy fire.

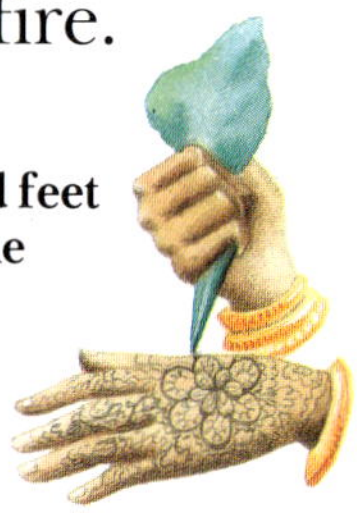

The bride's hands and feet are decorated with fine patterns traced in a vegetable dye called henna.

The groom lifts up the bride's veil; this may be the first time he has ever seen her. Weddings are splendid and cost a lot of money. The couple live in the groom's house, where the groom's mother rules the household.

The Ganges is a sacred river for all Hindus.

For Hindus, God has thirty-three million different forms. The three main forms are Brahma, Vishnu and Shiva. Children learn about them by hearing stories from the Ramayana and the Mahabharata, long tales all about the gods and their battles. The Ganges River is revered by all Hindus. They call it Ganga Mai, our mother Ganges. Hindus believe that, if you bathe in it, your sins will be washed away .

India is a land of festivals. There are feasts to celebrate the thousands of gods. Some feasts last for several days. Diwali is the festival of light. In the north they celebrate Diwali at the new year. Each house glimmers with thousands of tiny oil lamps, and children set off fireworks.

The festival of Holi is celebrated with flags and drums.

Hindus believe that after somebody dies, the soul is born again as some other living thing: a person, animal or insect. This is called reincarnation. They believe that if you die in Varanasi, a holy city on the banks of the Ganges, you will not have to be reincarnated again.

Japan: a string of over a thousand islands

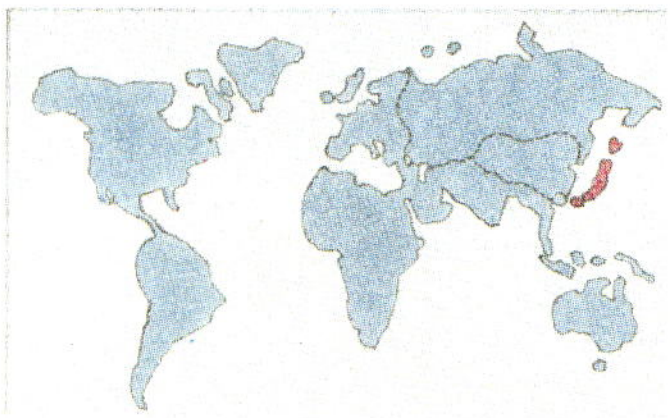

Land of the Rising Sun

According to Japanese tradition, 'where the sun bursts forth from the sea, there is Japan'.
The Japanese are also known as Nippons. In their language that means 'they who make the sun rise'. A bright red sun is the symbol of their country.

Japan is far to the east of Europe. When you're asleep, the Japanese are just waking up.
From north to south, there are almost 4,000 islands in the Japanese archipelago. Try to remember the names of the three biggest: snowy Hokkaido in the north, Honshu, the largest, home to Mount Fuji and the capital Tokyo, and Kyushu, to the south.

Japanese floors are covered with mats of woven cane. To keep them clean, you have to take off your shoes before going indoors.

Earthquakes* are usual in Japan.

Most of the time, they are little tremors that you can't even feel. But in the past, Japan has been rocked by some horrible earthquakes. The huge 1923 quake flattened most of Tokyo. Nowadays houses are made of wood and raised on pylons, to stand up to the shaking.

Tall buildings are also earthquake-proof, with special pylons that will sway but not fall over if the earth begins to move.
Everything in a Japanese house is light and easy to move. The windows don't have glass, and the inner walls are sliding screens made of squares of delicate rice paper.

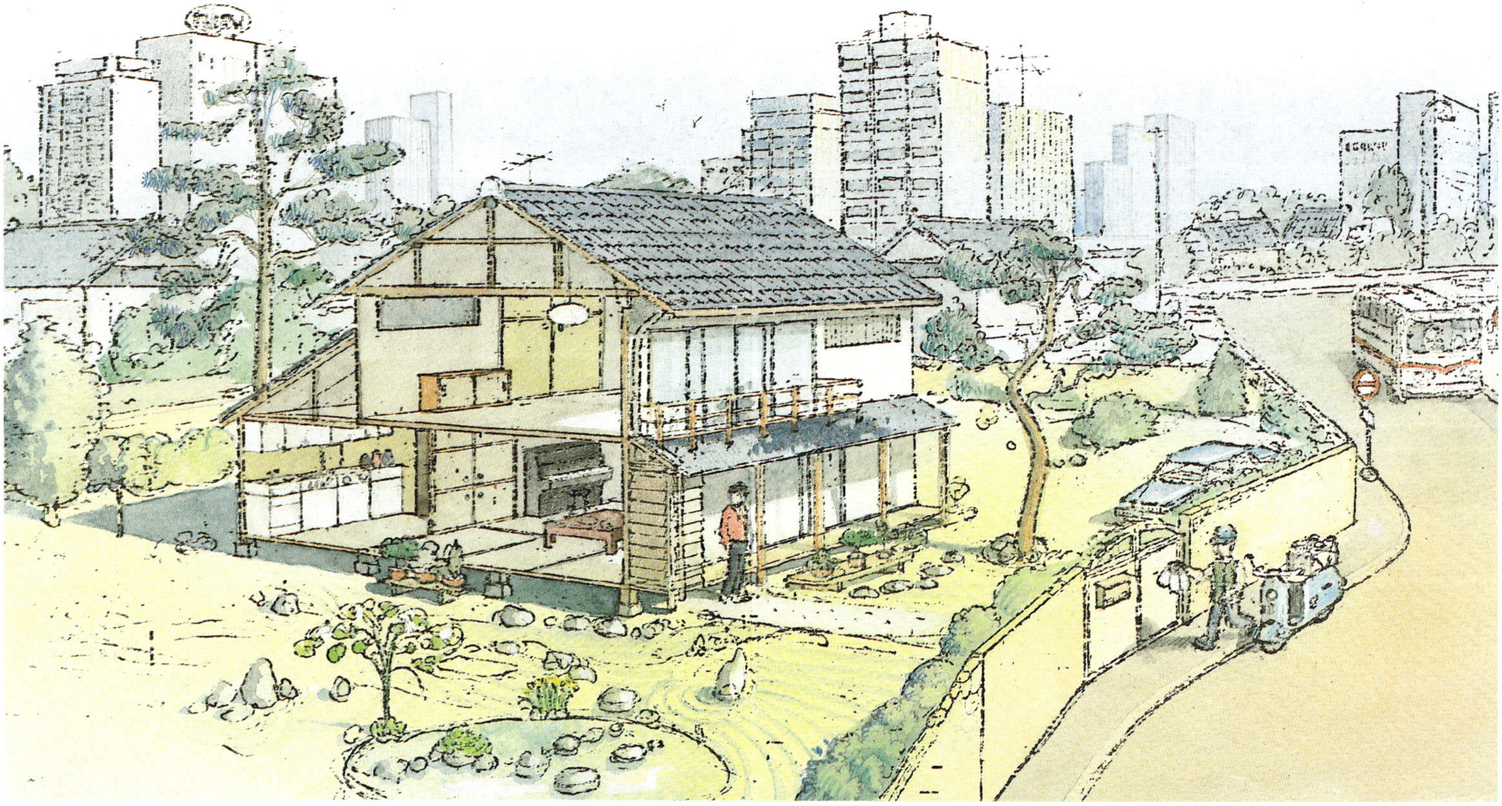

Ancient customs are part of daily life.

A plate of sushi, raw fish on a bed of rice

Fish is always on the menu in Japan.
The Japanese catch more fish than any other nation and eat three times more than we do. They often eat it raw, cut in cubes and dipped in a spicy sauce; this is sushi. They also enjoy seaweed, served as a vegetable or in soups. Don't look for a chair at a Japanese meal! Sit on a cushion on your knees, at a low table. There are no knives or forks either; use the chopsticks to pick up the cubes of food.

A festival kimono

Beds unroll and roll up again.
The futon, a cosy quilt with a mattress, is tucked away in the cupboard during the day. At night it is stretched out on the matted floor.

Futons save space, and are very comfortable to sleep on.

Japanese baths follow an ancient tradition.
The water is very hot, and the whole family bathes together. Whether they are at home or in the public bath, everyone soaps up and rinses off before they go into the tub or pool, so the communal water stays clean for the others.
The bathers climb out shiny and red, and very relaxed.

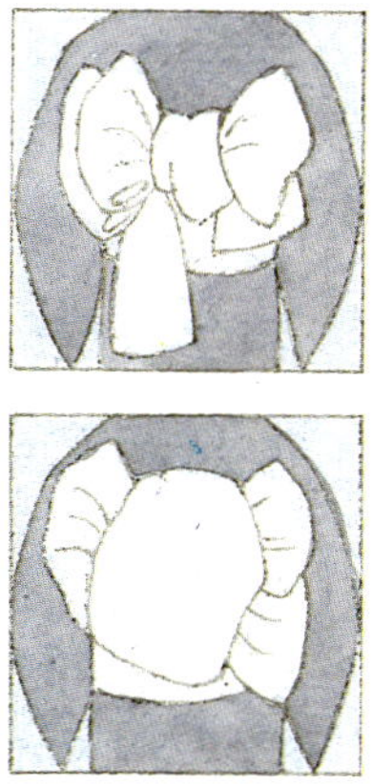

Two ways to tie an obi, the wide belt that holds a kimono (robe) in place.

Crowds rush and push through the busy streets of Tokyo.

During rush hour, pushers squeeze commuters into trains and force the doors closed.

Tokyo and its endless suburbs form one of Asia's busiest cities.
Crowds dash through the streets to work. In Tokyo, the streets have no proper names, and buildings have no real numbers. But somehow letters are delivered anyway!

Paintbrush and Chinese ink

How do you write in Japanese?
Not with the twenty-six letters of our alphabet, but with little drawings called characters. Each represents a word or an idea. There are several hundred thousand all together. To read well, you need to learn two thousand characters. To start with, children use forty-six symbols.

Great competitions between kites take place every year.
Festivals like these occur all over Asia. The kites are huge and beautifully decorated. It takes a whole team on the ground to manoeuvre a single kite. Thin strings that hold up the kite can cut your hands like glass. Each team tries to sever the lines of their opponents' kite. On this kite you can see the symbol of Japan, the red sun.

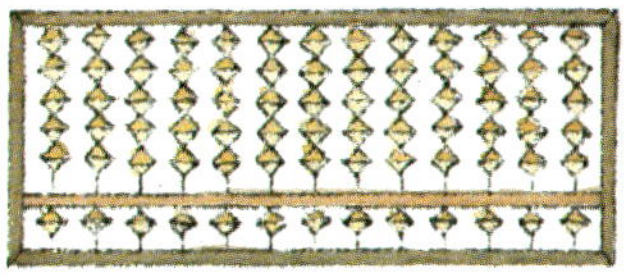

In the land of the calculator, many people still count with an abacus*.

Japan has two religions: Shintoism, born in Japan, and Buddhism, which came from India.
Shintoists worship many gods. This Shinto procession is moving towards a temple. Drums and cymbals guide the steps of the priests, who are carrying a statue of a god. Buddhists follow the teaching of a wise Indian monk who was given the name Buddha, or 'Enlightened One'.

One quarter of all the people living in the world are Chinese.

More people live in China than in any other country in the world.
There are more than one billion two hundred thousand people in China. Over nine million live in Beijing, the capital. From six o'clock in the morning, crowds fill the streets. Pedlars are everywhere selling their goods and services, one offering to repair your bike, another to clean your ears… Tiananmen Square, in the heart of the city, is the largest square in the world.

China is a great power.
It is also a very poor country. Every year the number of people increases by about 12 million. Only 15% of China's land can produce food, so it is a problem trying to feed everyone. This is why the government encourages couples to have only one child. It is common these days for a Chinese child to be an only child, with no brothers or sisters.

The Chinese love birds, and will often go for walks carrying caged birds with them.

Schools are very crowded.
Children have only had to go to school since 1985. Many people cannot read or write. For country families, it may seem more important for children to work in the fields, helping to bring in food for the family.

How do people get about in China?
Most people travel by bicycle. There are still very few cars. Peasants use carts pulled by donkeys to take their fruit and vegetables to market. The buses are always packed full of people, and they can only move very slowly through the crowds of cyclists.

Chinese, but also Tibetan, Mongol, Manchu...

The Dalai Lama*, the living god of the Tibetans, used to live in Potala, on the roof of the world, 7,000 metres above sea level.

From the high plateaux of Tibet to deserts and forests of bamboo.
There is every imaginable kind of landscape in China. And not everyone who lives there is Chinese. Tibetans, Manchus and Mongols also live in China, but the Chinese outnumber them all. The other peoples are ethnic minorities.

The panda is the national symbol of China.
Pandas live in bamboo forests. They eat just one type of bamboo, and there are not many pandas left. These huge black and white bears are extremely strong and have long, razor-sharp claws.

The Great Wall of China is so huge that it can be seen from the moon!
Building work was started on the Wall about 200 BC by the Qin Emperor Shi Huangdi, who wanted to keep out barbarian invaders coming in from the north.

In southern China, rice grown on terraces is harvested two or three times a year.

The Huang River (5,000 km long) floods often, and is called the Scourge of China. The Yangtze (5,800 km long) is safer.

In the tropical south of China, with palm trees and bamboo thickets, water buffalo help the peasants to till the rice fields.

The oasis of Turpan, in the middle of the north-eastern deserts, is famous for its beautiful Muslim mosque*.

The nomads* of Mongolia herd their horses and put up their yurts, tents of skin or felt, out on the frozen plain.

A tea-house in Shanghai

Tea is the national drink of China.
It was discovered by a Chinese emperor. The usual tea is green tea, bought in small packets. The Chinese drink tea at any hour of the day and night, but they don't add milk or sugar. They also like hot water. A thermos of boiled water is kept for drinking and making tea.

In the south, most people eat rice at every meal.
In north China, they prefer bread rolls or noodles made with egg and flour. When Marco Polo* visited China he discovered these noodles, and took some back to Italy with him. The Italians liked them so much that pasta soon became the national dish. The Chinese do not use butter or cheese. All the fresh milk is saved for the children. Grown-ups drink soya milk, which is made from soya beans. They often finish a meal with soup.

Suzhou, with its hundreds of canals, is called the Venice of China. It stands on the Grand Canal, which joins the Yangtze River to Beijing.

Chinese dishes: noodles, hundred-year eggs, shark fins, black mushrooms, roast duck, steamed buns, ginger…

Most Chinese live in the countryside.

An outdoor restaurant in Beijing. In the evening, parks and pavements are crowded with people taking a walk, talking to friends, playing board games. It is difficult to be alone in China.

Eight out of every ten Chinese people live in the country. The peasants work in the paddy-fields in their bare feet, up to their ankles in water. Children help their parents to tend pigs or ducks.

Islands in the ocean: Australasia, the fifth continent

On the opposite side of the world from London and New York is Australasia, which includes Australia, New Zealand, and the thousands of islands of Polynesia. Australia is a huge island nearly as big as the USA. Things seem back-to-front 'down under'. Daytime in Europe is night in Australia. The seasons are upside down too. Spring in Europe is autumn there. Can you imagine Christmas in the summer?

The Aborigines* were the first people to live in Australia. They came across the sea in prehistoric times. The first European settlers were British convicts sentenced to exile in Australia in 1788. When gold was discovered, in 1851, settlers came in large numbers from all over the world. They seized the homelands and sacred sites of the Aborigines.

Australia is the land of kangaroos, koalas and kookaburras.

The pioneers who settled Australia's outback* had to clear trees, build houses and boats and make roads. Then the farmers started to plant crops and establish huge herds of sheep and cattle.

Weird and wondrous desert-dwellers

The bird of paradise, a visitor from New Guinea

It looks fierce, but the thorny devil, a little dragon lizard, is no bigger than your hand and only eats ants. The blue-tongued lizard is about 45 cm long. Surprise it basking in the sun and it may hiss and stick out its tongue, but it's quite harmless. Listen! The loud cackle of laughter overhead is the kookaburra, 'merry, merry king of the bush is he'; a sound like a bell tinkling is the bell-bird; a soft low whistle followed by the sharp crack of a whip is the whipbird. The emu is one of the tallest birds in the world. It can't fly, but it can run very, very fast!

The wombat lives in a burrow like a badger. This plump, furry marsupial has strong paws and shovel-like claws for digging.

At dead of night an eerie howl shatters the silence, echoed by an answering howl further off. Dingoes call to each other. These wild dogs roam the land in small packs, hunting rabbits and other animals.

Kangaroos are the most famous of all Australia's marsupials.

When a baby kangaroo or 'joey' is born, it crawls straight into its mother's pouch. In a while it will venture out to eat grass, diving back into the pouch head first when frightened. Marsupials are animals whose babies are carried in a pouch on their mother's bodies for the first months of their lives. They come in all shapes and sizes, from wallabies and koalas to tiny marsupial mice that hop like kangaroos.

Long sandy beaches, wide open spaces

An outdoor life, even in the city
Australian cities are like any others: busy, noisy, filled with traffic. But because it is often fine, Australian children spend a lot of time outdoors. Schoolchildren eat packed lunches outside all year round. Even in mid-winter you can have a barbecue or a birthday party or your school sports day in the park, amongst the joggers and sunbathers.

Beyond the high buildings, you can catch sight of the deep blue ocean glittering in the sun.

On surfboards or in long rowing boats, lifesavers go to the rescue of a swimmer caught in the surf.

Beaches as far as the eye can see...
Australia has more beaches than any other country in the world. The sea never gets very cold, so people sail, swim and surf all year round, to say nothing of deep-sea diving, windsurfing and fishing. Australian children are good swimmers, but they are taught to stay close to shore. There may be dangerous currents, or even sharks.

The Australian bush begins where the city ends.
Bushwalking is a serious business. You must be prepared. You will need: tough shoes or boots, a hat, a backpack, water, a good map and a 'billy can' for brewing your tea.

Farmers in the outback live on stations, farms as big as counties.

The flying doctor pays a call. Stations have airstrips where small planes can land.

Can you imagine living so far out in the country that your nearest neighbours are several hours' drive away?

That is the Australian outback*, dry and endless. Farmers and their families live on huge 'stations', often hundreds of kilometres

apart. The roads are just dirt tracks. The 'jackaroos', or farm workers, used to round up the huge herds of sheep on horseback. But now they use motorbikes, trucks and even helicopters.

What about school?
Some children don't go to school – school comes to them, by radio. They do their work by tuning in to the 'School of the Air'.

The teachers may be many hundreds of kilometres away, but each pupil can talk to them as if they were together in one big classroom.

The farmhouse or homestead is designed to keep out the heat and the flies. Many houses stand on stilts as well, so that snakes can't get in. There are flyscreens on the doors and windows. Rainwater runs off the corrugated iron roof and is collected in rain tanks. Children soon learn to help around the station. Most of them have horses of their own and are good riders.

Kangaroos crossing!

Did you know that there are wonderful islands of palm trees and soft sand, set in warm, clear seas? They are tropical islands. The islands are like gardens, full of flowers and delicious fruit. Under the sea it is like a garden too; corals of every colour, and shells, and fish darting about!

The Tropics lie in the orange and red bands on the map, near the Equator*.

To show what tropical islands are like, we have chosen one island, called Nossy-Be. It lies north west of Madagascar, off the coast of Africa. In Malagasi, Nossy-Be means 'big island'.

There are many other tropical islands: Hawaii, Tahiti, the West Indies, the Galapagos Islands... They are all near the Equator*, between the Tropic of Cancer to the north and the Tropic of Capricorn to the south.

Houses are lifted above the ground on little stilts, so water cannot get into them in stormy weather.

Shark: best avoided, in case you end up as his meal!

Nearly everyone on these islands lives by fishing, there are so many delicious fish swimming in the waters around Nossy-Be!
Each fisherman makes his own canoe.
He finds a hardwood tree and cuts it down.
Then he hollows it out with a small axe.
To make the canoe more stable, he puts on a frame called an outrigger which balances it as it floats. The sail is a square of cotton.
On feast days, the young men race each other. The whole village lines up on the beach to watch.

Grouper

Ray

Going fishing

As soon as the sun is up, fishermen lay baskets rather like lobster-pots on the sea-bottom. By nightfall they will be full of little fish. Then the men pay out a net from the back of their canoes as they paddle towards the shore. When they draw in the net it is crammed with fish with strange-sounding names: thread-fin, barracuda, tiger-fish, parrot-fish. In no time at all they will all have been eaten, grilled or raw, soaked in coconut milk.
The easiest place to fish is in a lagoon*, separated from the open sea by a wall of brilliant coral. The water here is turquoise.

Barracuda

The fish are attached to poles to carry them up to the houses.

Bananas, coconuts and sugar cane thrive in the tropical sunshine.

Each family builds its own house. The walls are made of bamboo canes and banana leaves. The roof is covered with coconut palms.

In the middle of the island, sugar cane is grown in huge fields.

At the market: cinnamon sticks, mild and hot chillies, pineapples, all sorts of bananas, big and tiny, purple, green, yellow…

Spices for flavouring food

Cooking is usually done out of doors.
As well as fish cooked over open fires, there are lots of vegetables, salads and rice. Maniocs and yams grow underground like potatoes. The leaves of maniocs can be eaten as well. Turmeric, another root vegetable, has rather a strong taste. It is powdered and used for flavouring food.

Sugar and spice and all things nice…
Spices taste very strong. Just a little gives a good flavour to food. The strongest spices are red or green chillies. If you're not used to them, they make your mouth feel as if it's on fire!

Yams are eaten mashed or fried.

Manioc roots are grated and pressed.

Turmeric root

Vanilla is a precious spice.
The plant has a beautiful yellow flower. The fruit hangs in bunches of green pods, which grow dark and sweet-smelling as they dry. Vanilla ice-cream gets its flavour from these pods.

Children climb palm trees to fetch the coconuts that grow on them.
Every bit of a coconut is useful.
The clear 'milk' is like fresh water; the white flesh can be eaten by itself or used for making cakes, oil, candles, even soap – it's coconut oil which makes your skin go frothy. The hairy outside part is used to make mats, and the hard shells make good bowls.

Zebus are cow-like animals with a hump which stores fat.

Every year, from December to February, cyclones sweep across the island.
Cyclones are severe storms. Violent winds whip up the waves until they are higher than houses. Crops are flattened, trees uprooted, houses swept away…
After two or three days, the sun is out again.

Greenland: a land of ice in the far north, home to the Eskimos

Greenland, a frozen land within the Arctic* circle, is the biggest island in the world. The people who live there are Eskimos. They call themselves 'Inuit', which means 'the real people'. They live on the shores of the island, which are always covered in snow. Nobody lives inland; it is a huge ice-cap. In winter the sun barely rises over the horizon. There are places where the sun does not rise at all for months, and the night lasts for weeks on end.

A 'real person'

Eskimos live mainly by hunting and fishing, as it is too cold to grow any fruit or vegetables in the frozen ground. The villages are small, because there are not many people living in these cold places. The gaily painted houses brighten up the white landscape. Nowadays, almost all the villages have electricity.
The Eskimos hunt seals and polar bears. The skins are dried and kept outside in the icy air. There are almost twice as many dogs as there are people.

How do the Eskimos keep out the cold?
Wearing two pairs of boots, trousers made of bear-skin, and an anorak made of seal-skin or caribou hide, they go out even when it's –50°C. It never gets as cold as that for us!

The winter evenings are long and dark.

Kayaks* and sledges are laid across frames so that the hungry dogs won't chew the leather.

In the warm near the stove, which serves for both heating and cooking, the women tan hides while the men make harpoons. The children play games. They eat meat or fish, either dried or boiled, seal blubber, and rice. Their water comes from ice which is melted in a bucket. In early times the walls of their huts were covered in seal-skins to keep in the warmth. Not so long ago they were covered in newspapers – just as good at keeping in the heat, and much easier to catch!

This women is chewing a piece of seal leather to make it soft to sew.

A shop right in the middle of Greenland, selling all sorts of tools and supplies

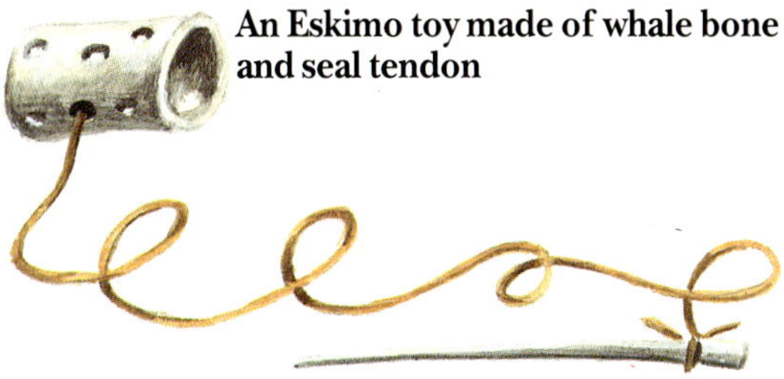

An Eskimo toy made of whale bone and seal tendon

Eskimos live in other countries too. Some make their homes in northern Canada, or in Alaska, a state of the USA, or in Siberia, in the far north of Russia. They don't all speak the same language, but they can usually understand each other.

Teams of dogs drag sledges across the ice.

It takes as many as fifteen dogs to pull a sledge. The leader is often a female, while the other dogs may be her grown-up puppies.

An Eskimo seal hunter hides behind a white screen held up by little skis. Only his gun pokes through as he creeps up on the seal.

Seals are very precious. They provide meat, blubber, oil, skins, bones for toys and tools, and tendons which are used as thread.

Hunting by kayak*. The kayak is a long, thin canoe, made of seal-skins stretched over a wooden frame. There is room for one person.

Eskimos have dogs to pull their sledges when they go out hunting or fishing.

A hunter going on an expedition needs to pack many things: a gun, an axe, a harpoon, a saw, a fur rug, a tent, a stove and pan, plenty of food. All this is tied to the sledge with seal-tendon rope. A team of dogs pulls the sledge, with the most intelligent dog in front as leader. The dogs are strong, and can pull heavy loads. Harnessed in a fan shape, each stays in its place. The master gives his orders to the leader. To make the dogs turn right, their master shouts "illi-illi", to make them go left, "ka-ka". Going downhill, the dogs are tied behind the sledge to slow it down.

The dogs sleep outside.

Their thick fur protects them from the cold as they lie curled up in the snow, their noses tucked under their tails. When they get up, they crack their way out of a shell of snow.

Shark fishing. The fisherman makes a hole in the ice and drops a line. When the shark takes the bait, he harpoons it and pulls it out of the water, where it freezes right away in the cold air.

How do you make an igloo?

When the hunters are too far from the village to return in the evening, they build a shelter in the snow: an igloo. They cut out big blocks of hard snow with a saw. In earlier times, they used a bone knife.

Inside an igloo, seen from above

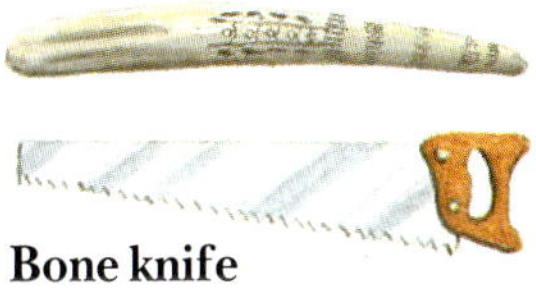

Bone knife
Snow saw

When the blocks are cut, they are piled like bricks one on top of the other, in a spiral shape like a snail's shell. The hardened blocks form an icy shelter that keeps out the wind and cold. But the light passes through the ice, so inside the igloo it is bright and cheerful. The hunters cut benches out of the hard snow so they can sit down. Then they light a fire and heat up some soup for dinner, inside their ice home! The smoke and fumes escape through a small hole in the roof.

Inside an igloo, from the side

Shark meat is not good to eat, but dried it can be fed to the dogs.

All around the world...

Next to each country is its capital.

EUROPE
1. Albania, Tirana
2. Austria, Vienna
3. Belgium, Brussels
4. Belorussia, Minsk
5. Bosnia-Hercegovina, Sarajevo
6. Bulgaria, Sofia
7. Croatia, Zagreb
8. Czech Republic, Prague
9. Denmark, Copenhagen
10. Estonia, Tallinn
11. Finland, Helsinki
12. France, Paris
13. Germany, Berlin
14. Greece, Athens
15. Hungary, Budapest
16. Iceland, Reykjavik
17. Ireland (Eire), Dublin
18. Italy, Rome
19. Latvia, Riga
20. Liechtenstein, Vaduz
21. Lithuania, Vilnius
22. Luxembourg Luxembourg
23. Moldavia, Kishinev
24. The Netherlands, Amsterdam
25. Norway, Oslo
26. Poland, Warsaw
27. Portugal, Lisbon
28. Romania, Bucharest
29. Russian Federation, Moscow
30. Slovakia, Brno
31. Slovenia, Ljubljana
32. Spain, Madrid
33. Sweden, Stockholm
34. Switzerland, Bern
35. Ukraine, Kiev
36. United Kingdom, London
37. Yugoslavia, Belgrade

AMERICA
38. Antigua & Barbuda, St Johns
39. Argentina, Buenos Aires
40. Bahamas, Nassau
41. Barbados, Bridgetown
42. Belize, Belmopan
43. Bolivia, La Paz
44. Brazil, Brasilia
45. Canada, Ottawa
46. Chile, Santiago
47. Colombia, Bogota
48. Costa Rica, San Jose
49. Cuba, Havana
50. Dominican Republic, Santo Domingo
51. Ecuador, Quito
52. Salvador, San Salvador
53. Guatemala, Guatemala City
54. Guyana, Georgetown
55. Haiti, Port-au-Prince
56. Honduras, Tegucigalpa
57. Jamaica, Kingston
58. Mexico, Mexico City
59. Nicaragua, Managua
60. Panama, Panama
61. Paraguay, Asuncion
62. Peru, Lima
63. Surinam, Paramaribo
64. Trinidad & Tobago, Port of Spain
65. United States of America, Washington
66. Uruguay, Montevideo
67. Venezuela, Caracas

AFRICA
68. Algeria, Algiers
69. Angola, Luanda
70. Benin, Porto Novo
71. Botswana, Gaborone
72. Burkina-Faso, Ouagadougou
73. Cameroon, Yaoundé
74. Central African Republic, Bangui
75. Chad, Ndjamena
76. Congo, Brazzaville
77. Egypt, Cairo
78. Equatorial Guinea, Malabo
79. Ethiopia, Addis Ababa
80. Gabon, Libreville
81. Gambia, Banjul
82. Ghana, Accra
83. Guinea, Conakry
84. Guinea-Bissau, Bissau
85. Ivory Coast, Yamoussoukro
86. Kenya, Nairobi
87. Lesotho, Maseru
88. Liberia, Monrovia
89. Libya, Tripoli
90. Madagascar, Antananarivo
91. Malawi, Lilongwe
92. Mali, Bamako
93. Mauritania, Nouakchott
94. Mauritius, Port Louis
95. Morocco, Rabat
96. Mozambique, Maputo
97. Namibia, Windhoek
98. Niger, Niamey
99. Nigeria, Abuja
100. Rwanda, Kigali
101. Senegal, Dakar
102. Sierra Leone, Freetown
103. Somalia, Mogadishu
104. South Africa, Pretoria
105. Sudan, Khartoum
106. Swaziland, Mbabane
107. Tanzania, Dodoma
108. Togo, Lomé
109. Tunisia, Tunis
110. Uganda, Kampala
111. Zaire, Kinshasa
112. Zambia, Lusaka
113. Zimbabwe, Harare

ASIA
114. Afghanistan, Kabul
115. Armenia, Yerevan
116. Azerbaijan, Baku
117. Bahrain, Manama
118. Bangladesh, Dhaka
119. Bhutan, Thimpu
120. Brunei, Bandar Seri Begawan
121. Burma, Rangoon
122. Cambodia, Phnom Penh
123. China, Beijing
125. India, New Delhi
126. Indonesia, Jakarta
127. Iran, Tehran
128. Iraq, Baghdad
129. Israel, Jerusalem
130. Japan, Tokyo
131. Jordan, Amman
132. Kazakhstan, Alma-Ata
133. Kirgizia, Bishkek
134. North Korea, Pyongyang
135. South Korea, Seoul
136. Kuwait, Kuwait
137. Laos, Vientiane
138. Lebanon, Beirut
139. Malaysia, Kuala Lumpur
140. Mongolia, Ulan Bator
141. Nepal, Katmandu
142. Oman, Muscat
143. Pakistan, Islamabad
144. Philippines, Manila
145. Qatar, Doha
146. Saudi Arabia, Riyadh
147. Singapore, Singapore
148. Sri Lanka, Colombo
149. Syria, Damascus
150. Taiwan, Taipei
151. Tajikistan, Dushanbe
152. Thailand, Bangkok
153. Turkey, Ankara
154. Turkmenistan, Ashkhabad
155. United Arab Emirates, Abu Dhabi
156. Uzbekistan, Tashkent
157. Vietnam, Hanoi
158. Yemen, San'a

AUSTRALASIA
159. Australia, Canberra
160. Fiji, Suva
161. New Zealand, Wellington
162. Papua New Guinea, Port Moresby

…six continents, five oceans, nearly two hundred countries

Games and activities, a quiz, intriguing facts, sayings, a glossary, followed by the index

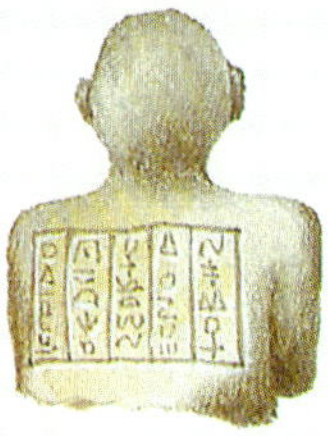

■ **Did you know?**

There are many different ways of writing.
Thousands of years ago, the ancient Egyptians were writing in hieroglyphics. These were eventually deciphered in 1822 by a French scholar, Jean-François Champollion. Some hieroglyphs are very simple pictures which represent what they show – a plant, animal or object. They are pictograms. Some peoples like the Chinese and the Japanese still write with pictograms today.

The Aborigines,
the first inhabitants of Australia, use four colours in their bark paintings: red and yellow, which are both made from ochre in the earth, white from chalk and black from charcoal.

Egyptian scribes – full-time writers – painted hieroglyphs on fine rolls of papyrus, a plant which still grows on the banks of the River Nile in Egypt.

This is the Milky Way Dreaming, a story often painted by the Aborigines. It tells how the universe was made.

The Tuareg people of the Sahara Desert
have their own language, tifinagh, with its own special alphabet. Children learn to read and write by drawing characters and forming sentences in the sand. This is how you write camel, tent, cow and teapot in tifinagh.

Learn how to draw four words in Japanese
ki = tree
té = hand
yama = mountain
hito = man

These four Japanese characters are all pictograms.
To draw them, you will need a long paintbrush which you dip in a special ink, Chinese ink.
Writing isn't just a way of communicating – it's also an art, called calligraphy.

How do you climb up on to a camel?
First you have to persuade it to get down on its knees – and that might take you quite a long time!
A camel moves its legs in pairs as it sways along, first the left ones, then the right. Riding on its back is like sitting in a boat on a very rough sea!

Camels tramp on endlessly across the desert. Their big feet prevent them from sinking into the sand. They can carry a load of 150 kilos, walk 50 km in one day, and go for several days without water. At the end of a journey, the camel has to drink a lot of water.
Camels are useful in many other ways too. Females provide milk, which is turned into camel cheese and camel yoghurt. Camel dung is burnt as fuel.

How do pygmies live?
Pygmies were the first inhabitants of central Africa. They live in the heart of the equatorial rainforest.
Few pygmies are more than 5 ft (1.5 m) tall. They know every plant in the forest; their houses are made from looped branches covered with overlapping leaves, and even their soap and toothpaste are made from plants.
Pygmies are famous for their medical skills.
Music and dance play an important part in their culture.

In India, women put on colourful make-up and glittering jewellery.

If a woman wears red powder in the parting of her hair, it means she is married.

Women also decorate their foreheads with a dot of red paint, a tika.
Peasant women wear heavy silver jewellery, day and night.

These jewels are worn by women in Rajasthan, in North-west India. In the towns, women prefer rings and bracelets of fine gold.

Do you know the martial arts?

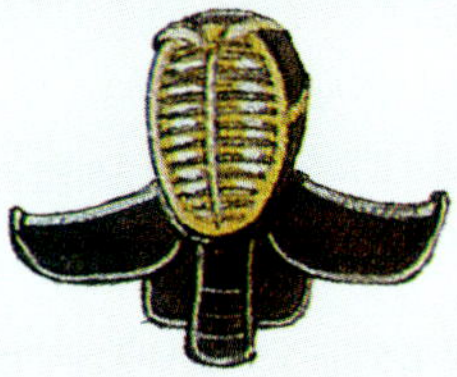

Samurai, Japanese warriors from the Middle Ages, knew many secret ways of fighting. Today these are known as the martial arts.

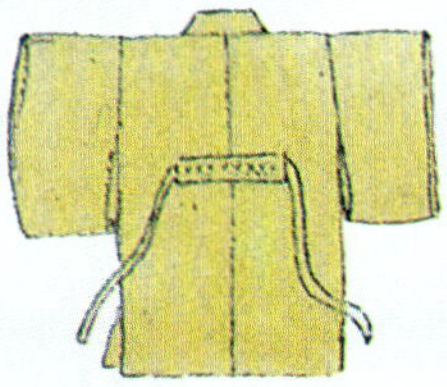

The martial arts are not just practised in Japan – these days they are popular in most countries, and are even part of the Olympics.

Kyodo is the Japanese art of archery. It takes great concentration to hold the bow, stretch the bowstring and aim at the target.

Kendo is a sort of fencing. The sword of long ago has been replaced with a long bamboo rod.

Sumo is part sport, part show business.
The Japanese love to watch sumo! It is a battle between two enormous wrestlers, 150 kilos of bulging muscle and fat. The aim of the game is to get a grip on your opponent and push him out of the circle on the floor. The struggle only lasts a few seconds. The great sumo wrestlers are great stars with many adoring fans.

Judo and judokas

There are no weapons in judo, just handholds and violent kicks.

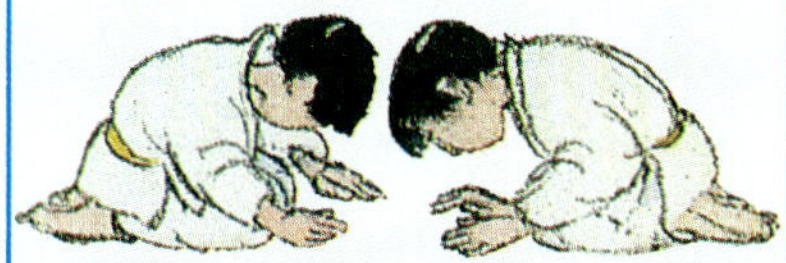

Before the struggle begins, the judokas bow to one other with great ceremony.

The colours of their belts show the level that each wrestler has reached. Beginners wear white or yellow belts, champions wear blue or, the ultimate, black belts.

The aim is to knock over your opponent and pin him or her on the ground. Doing this takes control and great concentration.

Karate is an art practised without weapons, like judo. It involves powerful blows of the hand.

■ Quiz

For each question, there is only one right answer. The correct answers are at the bottom of the page.

1. Which country produces the greatest number of feature films every year?
a) The USA
b) India
c) Italy

2. Which is the longest river in the world?
a) the Nile
b) the Amazon
c) the Mississippi

3. The currency of the USA is...
a) the yen
b) the dollar
c) the pound

4. The most popular game for children in Asia is...
a) baseball
b) cricket
c) flying kites

5. Chocolate was 'invented' by...
a) the Incas
b) the Chinese
c) the Tuareg

6. If you stuck a pin into a globe right through the centre of Britain, it would come out the other side in which country...
a) China
b) New Zealand
c) Brazil

7. The highest peak in Western Europe is in...
a) Austria
b) France
c) Scotland

8. The biggest football stadium in the world is found in...
a) Italy
b) Brazil
c) Texas

9. At 9 o'clock in the morning in London, what time is it in New York?
a) 2 o'clock in the afternoon
b) noon
c) 4 o'clock in the morning

10. The only country with wild camels is...
a) Mexico
b) Saudi Arabia
c) Australia

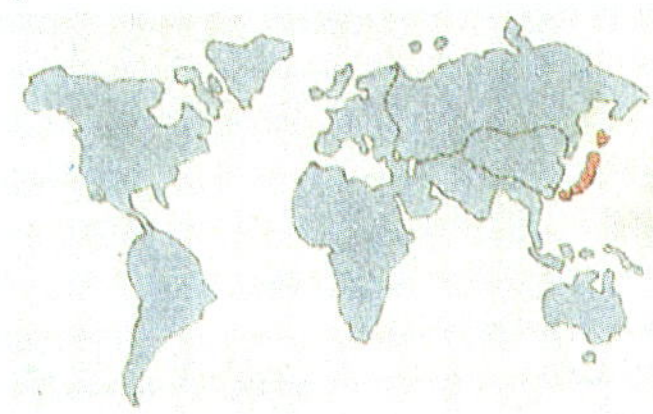

11. Tea is made from the tea plant's...
a) flowers
b) leaves
c) roots

12. Disneyland is in...
a) Florida
b) California
c) Florida and California

13. The European Community (EC) includes...
a) seven countries
b) twelve countries
c) all the countries of Europe

14. Canada's capital is...
a) Vancouver
b) Ottawa
c) Moose Jaw

Answers
1.b 2.a 3.b 4.c 5.a 6.b 7.b 8.b 9.c
10.c 11.b 12.b 13.b 14.b

Games and activities

Do you know how to throw a boomerang?
Getting it to come back is not easy!

Always throw a boomerang downwards as if you were aiming at the ground a few metres in front of you. Raise your arm and let the boomerang go as your arm comes down. It should loop round and up. But getting it right takes practice! Be careful not to throw a boomerang near houses or people – it is a dangerous weapon.

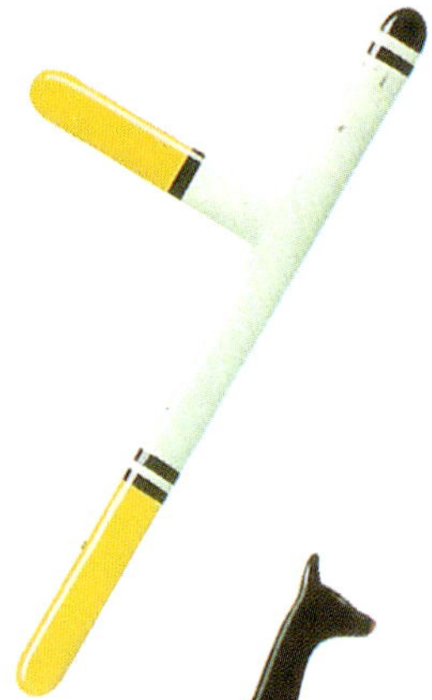

A collection of seashells from the Indian Ocean
There are hundreds of kinds of shells on the island of Nossy-Be. Children collect them in the lagoons and on the beach. After a swim, they lie in the shade of coconut palms, making necklaces out of shells, or using shells as counters in their games. At low tide you might even find the shell of a giant clam. When the clams are under the sea, their lips are a phosphorescent blue!

1, 2, 3 : cones;
4, 12 : murex;
5, 10, 11 : clams;
6, 7, 8, 9 : cowries

Giant clam

Not all boomerangs come back…
Australian Aborigines use returning boomerangs to drive game like kangaroos into nets, and then use non-returning boomerangs to kill them.

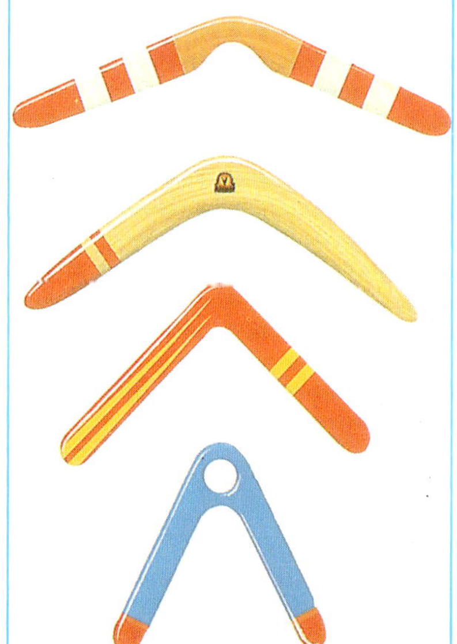

Make a club sandwich, a meal between two slices of bread!

First toast the bread. Smear one slice with mayonnaise and cover it with slices of cold roast chicken. Add a leaf of lettuce, a slice or two of bacon, a few pieces of tomato. Finally top it with the other slice of toasted bread.
The club is an American classic.

Landscapes of sand

On the north coast of Brazil, in the rolling dunes, people collect sand in every colour imaginable. Some artists fill bottles very meticulously with grains of different colours, using needles and spatulas and endless patience to create complicated pictures and landscapes in the sand.

French children play this game. Can you play it?

Each player will need :
6 matches (for the legs and eyes), 1 round piece of potato and 2 whole cloves (for the nose), 1 piece of macaroni (for the tail), 2 triangles of cardboard (for the ears), 1 big potato (for the body) and 1 small one (for the head).

Each player throws the dice in turn.
The points you roll allow you to put together your pig.
6 = tail, 5 = body, 4 = nose, 3 = eye, 2 = ear, 1 = leg.
The first to make a pig, wins the game!

A Japanese meal

The Japanese chop their meat, fish and vegetables into small cubes, which are easy to pick up with chopsticks.

Soya sauce

Tofu (bean curd)

They prepare a lot of fish raw, soaking it in vinegary sauces. Then they eat it dipped in soya sauce mixed with green mustard. All meals are accompanied by rice and green tea, drunk without milk.

Japanese cakes

Presentation is important in Japanese cooking. Food is eaten off beautiful plates of lacquered wood, colourful ceramics, even plastic... Cooks take courses to learn how to arrange food and decorate plates.

■ Glossary

Abacus: a Chinese invention to help you do sums quickly. Most shop assistants in China use one.
Aborigines: the first Australians, who came over the sea from Asia in prehistoric times. Many still live in the bush as their ancestors did.
Arctic: the frozen north. Parts of Canada, Alaska, Russia, Norway and all of Greenland are within the Arctic Circle, north of 60 degrees latitude.

Cartography: the art and science of drawing maps. Early cartographers were not able to get accurate information about unknown parts of the world, so their maps did not show the world as it really is.
Civilization: the culture and way of life developed by a people over centuries.
Conquistadores: Spanish conquerors who overcame the Indians of South and Central America in the 16th century. Their leaders were Cortés, who conquered the Aztecs in Mexico, and Pizarro who destroyed the Incas in Peru.

Dalai Lama: a living god and spiritual leader of the Tibetans. Since China invaded Tibet in 1950, the Dalai Lama has lived in exile in India.
Dreamtime: stories told by the Australian Aborigines for many generations, about the beginning of the world and the adventures of the first people.
Dromedary: a one-humped camel, the kind found in Africa, Arabia and wild in Australia. The two-humped or Bactrian camel is native to the cold deserts of China and Mongolia.

Earthquake: a violent shaking of the Earth's surface, caused by huge movements along fault lines in the Earth's crust. Certain parts of the world suffer frequent earthquakes, such as Japan, the west coast of the USA, and parts of Asia.
Emigrant: someone who leaves their own country to settle in another country.
Equator: an imaginary line running around the middle of the Earth. Near the equator the climates tend to be hot and sticky, and summer and winter are almost identical.

Gaucho: cowboy of South America. Gauchos ride the pampas (grasslands) rounding up cattle.

Hindi: the national language of India. Many Indians also speak English, or one of five hundred local dialects.

Immigrant: someone who comes to settle in a country permanently.
Irrigation: watering the fields artificially, instead of waiting for it to rain. This can be done with canals, electric pumps, sprinklers, reservoir water – even by changing the course of rivers.

Kayak: an Inuit canoe made of seal-skin stretched over a frame of driftwood, made for one passenger.

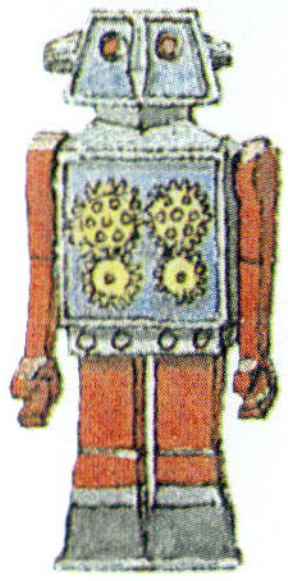

Umiaks are larger boats that can carry six or eight people.

Lagoon: a calm lake of salty water, separated from the open sea by a sandbank or coral reef.

Machete: a broad, heavy knife which is used in Central America and the West Indies as a tool and a weapon.
Marco Polo: an Italian traveller who visited China in the 13th century. He returned to Venice full of fantastic tales of the great civilizations of the east. One of the novelties he brought back to Italy with him was pasta.
Mosque: a Muslim church. Muslims pray here every day, going down on their knees facing Mecca, their holy city.

Nomads: wandering people who have no fixed home. Nomads usually live in tents which they pack up and carry with them on the backs of their horses or camels, or on their own backs.
North Pole: the most northerly point on Earth, at the icy centre of the Arctic Circle. The South Pole is at the other extreme of the Earth, in the middle of the freezing Antarctic continent.

Oasis: a little paradise in the desert. In some parts of the Sahara, springs of water flow near the surface, creating green islands in the desert.
Outback: the Australian bush, ranging from scrub to arid desert. Kangaroos roam the outback, where the few people live on stations, huge farms.

Savanna: the grasslands of Africa, where some of the largest mammals live. There are few trees and little shade.
The savanna is similar to the grasslands of the American prairies, the Argentine pampas and the Russian steppes.
Siesta: in hot countries of southern Europe, people take a rest, or siesta, after lunch when the sun is high in the sky.
After an hour or two, they get up again and continue working.
Slum: a very run-down district of a town or city, where very poor people live, often in rough and crowded conditions.
Steppe: a flat, grassy plain in eastern Europe, Russia and Siberia, where no trees grow. It is cold in winter.

Taoism: a Chinese religion. Taoists believe everything in nature is a balance between yin and yang, male and female, hot and cold, inside and outside.
Tundra: a huge, flat area in the Arctic, where the subsoil (the soil below the surface) is always frozen and there are no trees.

Here is a list of museums you could visit.
Your local library will help you find the addresses of other places you could go to find out more about the way people live all around the world.

Victoria and Albert Museum
Cromwell Road
London SW7

Museum of Mankind
6 Burlington Gardens
London W1

British Museum
Great Russell Street
London WC1

The Africa Centre
38 King Street
London WC2

Commonwealth Institute
Kensington High Street
London W8

London Museum of Jewish Life
80 East End Road
London N3

Pitt Rivers Museum
South Parks Road, Oxford

Ashmolean Museum
Beaumont Street, Oxford

Fitzwilliam Museum
Trumpington Street
Cambridge

Royal Museum of Scotland
Chambers Street
Edinburgh EH1 1JF

72

INDEX

The entries in **bold** refer to whole chapters on the subject.